A Bridge Goes Over

Kylie Burns
Crabtree Publishing Company
www.crabtreebooks.com

Be An Engineer!

Designing to Solve Problems

Author: Kylie Burns

Series research and development:
Janine Deschenes and Reagan Miller

Editorial director: Kathy Middleton

Editors: Petrice Custance, Crystal Sikkens

Proofreader: Janine Deschenes

Design: Katherine Berti

Photo research: Crystal Sikkens

Production coordinator and prepress technician:
Tammy McGarr

Print coordinator: Margaret Amy Salter

Photographs:

iStock: vm pp16, 18, 19; © narvikk p22

Keystone: ROPI via ZUMA Press pp14—15 (bottom)

Shutterstock: © Edwin Verin p7 (top right); © Remizov p13 (bottom);
© Jon Nicholls Photography p17

Superstock: Iain Masterton / age fotostock p 14 (inset)

Thinkstock: Noel Hendrickson p4

Wikimedia Commons: Tysto p12; Noodle snacks p 13 (top);
Tim Kiser p13 (middle); Barney Elliott p19 (computer inset)

All other images by Shutterstock

Animation and digital resources produced for
Crabtree Publishing by Plug-In Media

Library and Archives Canada Cataloguing in Publication

Burns, Kylie, author
A bridge goes over / Kylie Burns.

(Be an engineer! designing to solve problems)
Issued in print and electronic formats.
Includes index.
ISBN 978-0-7787-2907-5 (hardcover).--
ISBN 978-0-7787-2942-6 (softcover).--
ISBN 978-1-4271-1854-7 (HTML)

1. Bridges--Juvenile literature. 2. Bridges--Design and construction--
Juvenile literature. I. Title.

TG148.B87 2017   j624.2   C2016-907069-7
C2016-907070-0

Library of Congress Cataloging-in-Publication Data

Names: Burns, Kylie, author.
Title: A bridge goes over / Kylie Burns.
Description: New York, New York : Crabtree Publishing Company, [2017] |
Series: Be an engineer! Designing to solve problems | Audience: Ages 7-10.
| Audience: Grades 4 to 6. | Includes index.
Identifiers: LCCN 2016055769 (print) | LCCN 2016056169 (ebook) |
ISBN 9780778729075 (reinforced library binding : alk. paper) |
ISBN 9780778729426 (pbk. : alk. paper) |
ISBN 9781427118547 (Electronic HTML)
Subjects: LCSH: Bridges--Design and construction--Juvenile literature. |
Bridges--Juvenile literature.
Classification: LCC TG148 .B87 2017 (print) | LCC TG148 (ebook) | DDC
624.2--dc23
LC record available at https://lccn.loc.gov/2016055769

Crabtree Publishing Company

www.crabtreebooks.com   1-800-387-7650

Printed in Canada/032017/BF20170111

Published in Canada
Crabtree Publishing
616 Welland Ave.
St. Catharines, Ontario
L2M 5V6

Published in the United States
Crabtree Publishing
PMB 59051
350 Fifth Avenue, 59th Floor
New York, New York 10118

Published in the United Kingdom
Crabtree Publishing
Maritime House
Basin Road North, Hove
BN41 1WR

Published in Australia
Crabtree Publishing
3 Charles Street
Coburg North
VIC 3058

Contents

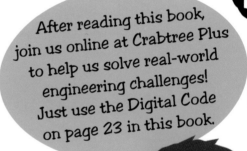

Hi, I'm Ava and this is Finn. Get ready for an inside look at the world of engineering! The Be an Engineer! series explores how engineers build structures to solve problems.

After reading this book, join us online at Crabtree Plus to help us solve real-world engineering challenges! Just use the Digital Code on page 23 in this book.

Crossing Over

Keisha always looks forward to visting her grandparents, but she doesn't enjoy the drive to their house. There is always heavy traffic, which makes the drive around the small lake take a very long time. Keisha wonders if there is a way to make the drive to her grandparents' house quicker.

Problem Solved!

Keisha began thinking, "what about using a train to take people around the lake, or using boats to carry people across? Could the lake be filled in so people could drive across it?" Then she thought of the perfect solution—a bridge! A bridge would allow people to drive across and keep the lake as it is.

What Is an Engineer?

People who enjoy solving problems, such as Keisha, think like engineers. An engineer is a person who uses math, science, and creative thinking to design things that solve problems and meet needs.

All Kinds of Engineers

There are many different kinds of engineers, including some who create roads, spaceships, buildings and structures, and even medicine. Not all engineers are the same. Some engineers design the materials for structures such as bridges. Others design the shape and size of a bridge. Most engineers work as part of a team.

Engineers discover new ways to improve our lives. The next time you ride in a car, eat an ice cream cone, or turn on a light, thank an engineer!

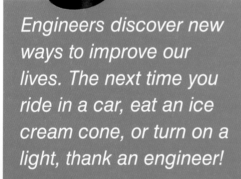

How Do Engineers Solve Problems?

Problems aren't always easy to solve. There are many steps engineers take to solve a problem. All engineers follow the same set of steps, called the Engineering Design Process. The steps in this process can be repeated over and over until the solution is both safe and **effective**. Making mistakes is often part of this process.

1 ASK

Ask questions and gather information about the problem you are trying to solve.

2 BRAINSTORM

Work with a group to come up with different ideas to solve the problem. Choose the best solution.

The Engineering Design Process

5 COMMUNICATE

Share your design with others.

3 PLAN AND MAKE A MODEL

Create a plan to carry out your solution. Draw a diagram and gather materials. Make a **model** of your solution.

4 TEST AND IMPROVE

Test your model and record the results. Using the results, improve, or make your design better. Retest your improved design.

Asking Questions

Engineers ask questions to gather information about the problem they need to solve. This is the first step in the Engineering Design Process. If an engineer needs to build a bridge across a river, it is important to find out what the usual weather is like in the area, and how much weight the bridge will need to hold.

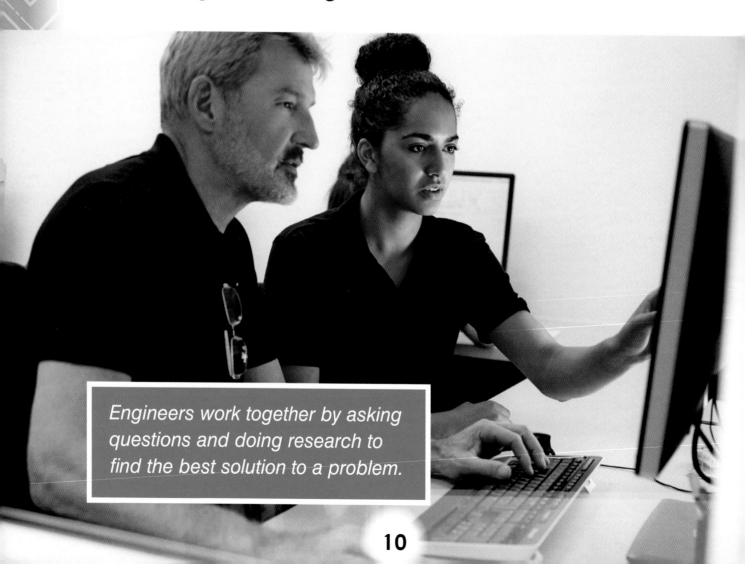

Engineers work together by asking questions and doing research to find the best solution to a problem.

Brainstorming

Once engineers have gathered their information, they brainstorm, or discuss possible solutions to the problem with others.

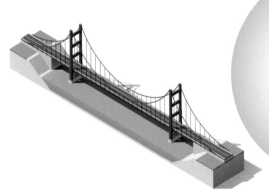

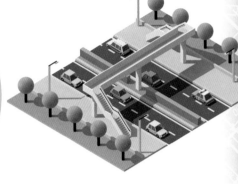

Build a bridge across the lake

Use a boat to transport people across the water

Problem
Heavy traffic makes driving around a small lake take too long

Fly people across the lake in an airplane

Build more roads so people can drive around the lake without getting stuck in traffic

Engineers may use a diagram like this to keep track of ideas when brainstorming.

Planning

If engineers decide a bridge is the best solution to their problem, they must decide what kind of bridge to build. There are many types of bridges to choose from, including suspension, arch, cantilever, and beam. Engineers make their choice based on things such as the span, or distance, the bridge will need to cross, how heavy the load on the bridge will be, and what kind of weather is normal in the area.

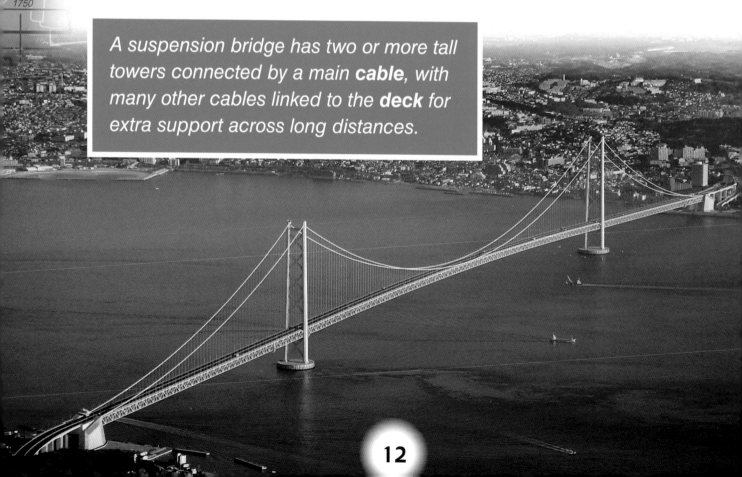

*A suspension bridge has two or more tall towers connected by a main **cable**, with many other cables linked to the **deck** for extra support across long distances.*

An arch bridge is made of one or more arches that give strong support to the deck.

A **beam** bridge has a flat beam stretching across two or more posts. This type of bridge is used for short distances.

A cantilever bridge is used for long distances. It is built with strong **piers** that support beams on each side.

Creating a Model

Once engineers know what kind of bridge they are going to build, they make a model of it. A model is a **representation** of the real bridge. Engineers can use their model to explain their design to others.

*A model is often designed on a computer or made as a **3-D** object.*

Testing and Improving

Engineers can also use their model to test the design of the bridge. Performing tests will tell engineers if there are areas in their design that need fixing or improving. After each test, engineers record the results and make improvements to their model. They repeat the tests until the model confirms the design is safe and effective.

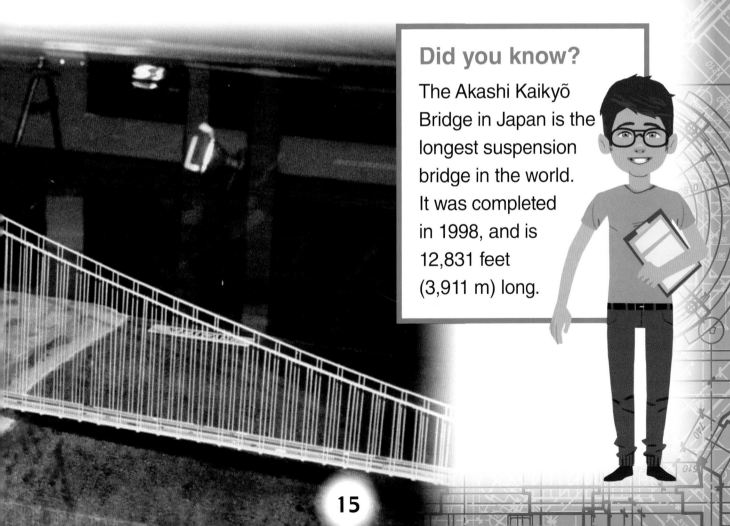

Did you know?

The Akashi Kaikyō Bridge in Japan is the longest suspension bridge in the world. It was completed in 1998, and is 12,831 feet (3,911 m) long.

Sharing the Results

The last step in the Engineering Design Process is for engineers to share their results. This allows engineers to learn from each other and help make sure bridges are built safely. By sharing results, engineers have improved the design of bridges to make them last longer and be more **stable**.

Then and Now

In the past, people got from place to place by walking or using horses. This means that early bridges were not built to hold a lot of weight. The invention of vehicles, such as trains, cars, and trucks, challenged engineers to come up with stronger bridge designs. By sharing these designs, engineers around the world were soon designing bridges capable of holding heavy vehicles.

Did you know?

Some engineers today have designed bridges with special equipment to create electricity, or power, using energy from the Sun!

Engineers are always improving or changing bridge designs to solve new problems, such as creating bridges that split so tall ships can get past.

Step by Step

The safety of people's lives depends on the proper design and building of a bridge. It is very important that engineers closely follow each step in the Engineering Design Process. Using this process correctly can help prevent a disaster from happening.

Bridge Failure

On November 7, 1940, the Tacoma Narrows Bridge in Tacoma, Washington, collapsed. At the time, it was the third-longest suspension bridge in the world. The engineers did not realize how strong the winds could get in that area. The winds caused one of the bridge's cables to snap, and eventually the whole bridge fell. Thankfully, no one was harmed.

How could using the Engineering Design Process have prevented the Tacoma Narrows Bridge disaster?

Model Activity

Using a model to test a bridge design is a very important step in the Engineering Design Process. It allows engineers to make sure their bridge can stand up to bad weather, such as strong winds, and be able to hold the correct amount of weight. Try it out for yourself by making and testing a model of a bridge.

You will need:

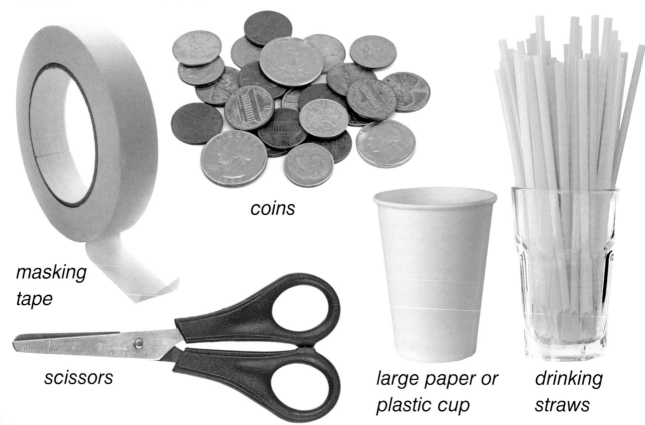

masking
tape

coins

scissors

large paper or
plastic cup

drinking
straws

Instructions

1. Arrange three straws side by side, each about 2 inches (5 cm) apart. Ask an adult to help you cut two straws to fit across both ends of the three straws. Use tape to secure the straws together. Repeat this process and tape the sets of straws together. You can make your bridge as long as you wish by adding more sets of straws.

2. Arrange your straw bridge across two desks or two stacks of books that are spaced apart. Put some coins in the cup and place it on the bridge.

- Did your bridge hold? If so, try adding a few more coins to the cup. If it didn't hold, how do you think you could strengthen your bridge?

Avoiding Disaster

The Tacoma Narrows Bridge disaster happened almost 80 years ago. Since then, safety procedures, or steps, have been put in place to help prevent disasters from happening. Today, research and designs of bridges are shared with a team of engineers. This way, errors or problems not seen by one engineer might be caught by others before the bridge is built.

Once a bridge is built, engineers must check it regularly to make sure it does not have weak areas and has not been damaged.

Learning More

Books

Briscoe, Diana. *Bridge Building; Bridge Designs and How They Work*. Red Brick Learning, 2005.

May, Vicky. *3-D Engineering: Design and Build Your Own Prototypes.* Nomad Press, 2015.

Novak, Patty O'Brien. *Engineering the ABC's: How Engineers Shape Our World.* Fern Press, 2009.

Websites

Test your skills on the bridge-design challenge here: **www.pbs.org/wgbh/buildingbig/ bridge/basics.html**

Visit this site for cool facts about bridges: **www.easyscienceforkids.com/ all-about-bridges/#**

For fun engineering challenges, activities, and more, enter the code at the Crabtree Plus website below.

www.crabtreeplus.com/be-an-engineer

Your code is:
bae04

Glossary

Note: Some boldfaced words are defined where they appear in the book.

3-D (THREE-DEE) *adjective* Short for three-dimensional, an object that has length, width, and height

beam (beem) *noun* A long, heavy piece of wood or metal that is supported at both ends

cable (KEY buh l) *noun* A strong and heavy rope, usually made of metal

deck (dek) *noun* The part of a bridge that is traveled across

effective (ih-FEK-tiv) *adjective* Producing the correct result

model (MOD-l) *noun* A representation of a real object

pier (peer) *noun* The upright posts that support the deck of a bridge

stable (STEY-buh-l) *adjective* Does not change position

representation (rep-ri-zen-TEY-shun) *noun* Something that stands in place for something else

A noun is a person, place, or thing. An adjective is a word that tells you what something is like.

Index